Written by Dawn Sirett
Illustrated by Rachael Hare, Louise Dick, Karen Hood,
Kitty Glavin, Victoria Palastanga, Kate Bull, Anna Kluska
Educational Consultant Penny Coltman
US Senior Editor Shannon Beatty
Designed by Rachael Hare, Louise Dick, Karen Hood,
Charlotte Bull, Polly Appleton, Victoria Palastanga, Claire Patane
Additional Editorial Work Sally Beets
Additional Design Work Jaileen Kaur,
Rajesh Singh Adhikari, Rajdeep Singh
Managing Editor Penny Smith
Managing Art Editor Mabel Chan
Producer, Pre-production Nadine King
Producer Inderjit Bhullar

First American Edition, 2018
Published in the United States by DK Publishing
345 Hudson Street, New York, New York 10014

Copyright © 2018 Dorling Kindersley Limited
DK, a Division of Penguin Random House LLC
18 19 20 21 22   10 9 8 7 6 5 4 3 2 1
001–308474–Sep/2018

A catalog record for this book
is available from the Library of Congress.
ISBN 978–1–4654–7084–3

DK books are available at special discounts when purchased in bulk
for sales promotions, premiums, fund-raising, or educational use.
For details, contact: DK Publishing Special Markets,
345 Hudson Street, New York, New York 10014
SpecialSales@dk.com

Printed and bound in China

A WORLD OF IDEAS:
SEE ALL THERE IS TO KNOW

www.dk.com

1000 Useful WORDS

tweet! tweet!

DK

Some useful words for parents

This book can be used with children who have not yet learned to read and with beginner readers. Each picture-packed page is fun to read together, and a great way to help children's language and literacy skills.

Picture-and-word pages

Most of this book is made up of picture-and-word pages filled with nouns, plus some verbs and adjectives. These pages help broaden your child's vocabulary and knowledge.

Story pages

There are also five simple stories to read that introduce more useful words, put words into context, and help sentence writing and story writing skills.

How to help your child get the most out of this book

All the pages in this book offer lots of opportunities for talking and learning. Enjoy exploring and talking about them together. Point out things your child likes. For instance, you could say, "Look, there's a tiger! Can you roar like a tiger?" or "Which fruit do you like?"

Go at your child's pace. Let her take the lead and turn the pages. Stop if she is tired, and return to the book another time.

For children who are not yet reading
Point to the pictures as you read the words and sentences to help them identify things, and to show how the pictures and words are connected.

For children who are beginning to read
As they read, or as you read together, point to the words, or encourage them to point, to help their letter and word recognition.

Following the stories
Pre-readers and beginner readers can follow the stories by running a finger along the dotted lines. This helps their fine motor skills, too.

"Can you find?" games and simple questions
There are "Can you find?" games and simple questions on the picture-and-word pages that encourage learning. Your child may need help with these, or he may like you to join in and answer with him.

Most importantly, follow your child's interests, talk about things you know he enjoys, give lots of praise as he answers the questions, and have fun!

A note about high-frequency words

High-frequency words, or sight words, are words that occur most often in books and other writing. Many are not nouns, verbs, or adjectives, but they are useful words such as "the," "and," "it," "I," and so on.

When children begin to read at school, they learn high-frequency words because these words will help them make sense of a sentence. Since quite a few can't be sounded out, children practice learning them by sight.

This book contains some high-frequency words, particularly in the question text and story pages. A list of Fry's first 100 high-frequency words is below. The 100 words are in frequency order.

the	or	will	number
of	one	up	no
and	had	other	way
a	by	about	could
to	words	out	people
in	but	many	my
is	not	then	than
you	what	them	first
that	all	these	water
it	were	so	been
he	we	some	called
was	when	her	who
for	your	would	oil
on	can	make	sit
are	said	like	now
as	there	him	find
with	use	into	long
his	an	time	down
they	each	has	day
I	which	look	did
at	she	two	get
be	do	more	come
this	how	write	made
have	their	go	may
from	if	see	part

Contents

Me and my body

What color are your **eyes**?
Is your **hair** long or short?

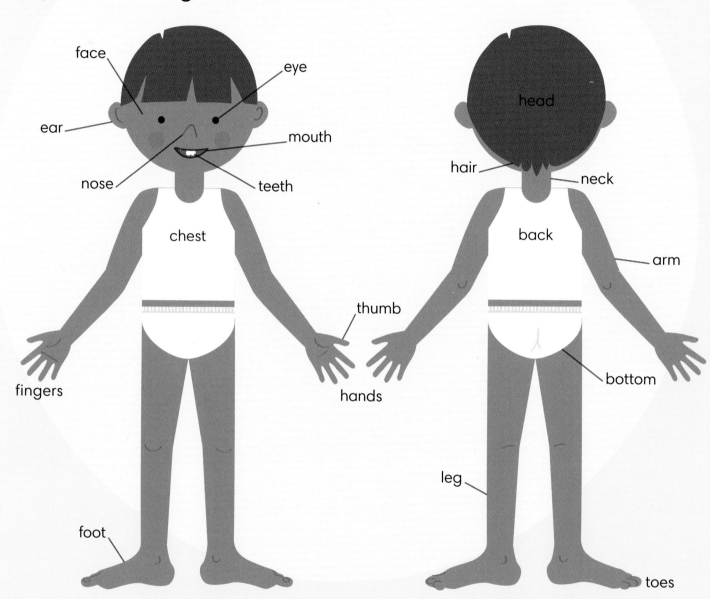

face

eye

ear

mouth

nose

teeth

chest

back

arm

thumb

fingers

hands

head

hair

neck

bottom

leg

foot

toes

Taking care of myself

hairbrush

soap

shampoo

sunblock

toothbrush

tissues
(for blowing
my nose!)

Things I do

I can...

sit

stand

walk

chatter! chatter!

talk

listen

laugh

jump

dance

roll

stretch

balance

bend

stomp

clap

wave

My senses

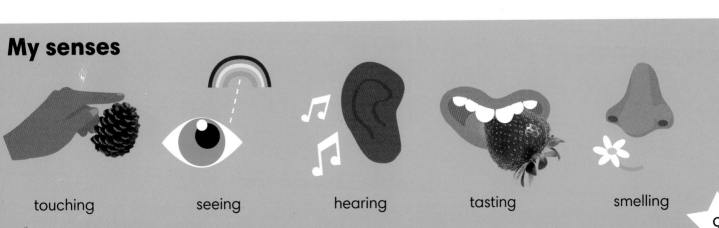

touching

seeing

hearing

tasting

smelling

My family and friends

There are all kinds of **families**...

I **love** my family.

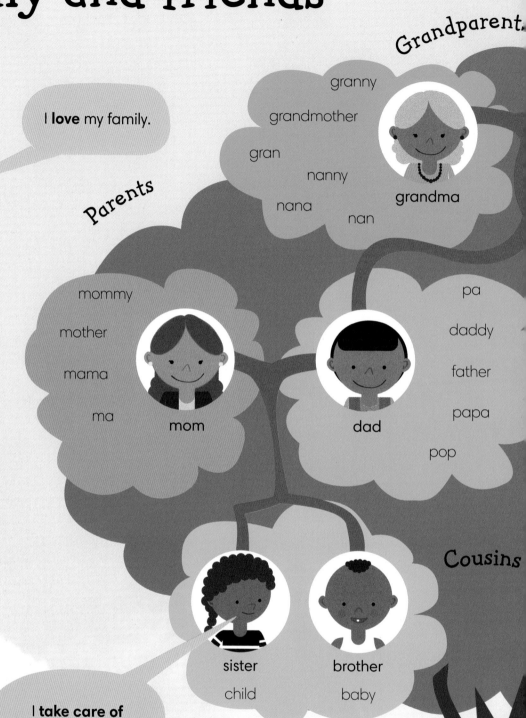

Grandparents

granny

grandmother

gran

nanny

nana

nan

grandma

Parents

mommy

mother

mama

ma

mom

pa

daddy

father

papa

pop

dad

Cousins

sister

child

brother

baby

Siblings

I **take care of** my little brother.

Who is the **oldest** person in your family?

grandad

grandfather

grandpop

grandpa

gramps

Relatives

pets

rabbit cat dog

I **love** my friends.

friends

aunt

auntie

uncle

twins

son

nephew

son

nephew

daughter

niece

Children

Things to wear

T-shirt

tank top

socks

tights

underpants

jeans

skirt

shorts

sweater

sun hat

watch

slippers

boots

gloves

woolen hat

scarf

sneakers

shoes

woolen hat

scarf

snowflake

Look at all the things **hanging** on the **clotheslines**. Choose something to wear on a **cold** day and...

button

dress

pants

fleece

umbrella

jacket

pajama top

swimming shorts

swimsuit

goggles

bag

pajama bottoms

necklace

backpack

zipper

belt

buckle

purse

baseball cap

bicycle helmet

dress-up clothes

sandals

hair bow

barrette

something to wear
on a **hot** day.

sunglasses

sun

13

Food and drink

What **vegetables** have you eaten today?

Fruit

grapes

pineapple

banana

apple

lemon

watermelon

strawberries

orange

Vegetables

potatoes

green beans

cauliflower

carrot

red pepper

onions

pumpkin

peas

cabbage

broccoli

Treats

cookies

cupcakes

pastries

ice cream

Choose three of these foods to make a **salad**.

tomato

cucumber

olives

lettuce

celery

In the fridge

cheese

chicken

eggs

butter

fish

sausages

yogurt

honey

bread

rice

cereal

noodles

pasta

oil

flour

tea

sugar

nuts

coffee

milk

spices

water

juice

In the pantry

Drinks

Choose one of these foods to make for **lunch**.

hamburger

sandwich

omelet

pizza

Find something healthy for your **snack box**.

15

All in a day

morning

alarm clock

bedside table

bed

Jack wakes up at **8 o'clock**.

Jack eats some **oatmeal** and a **banana** for **breakfast**.

breakfast time

toy carrot

oatmeal

banana

His **toy rabbit** has **food**, too!

hat

jacket

T-shirt

shorts

scarf

socks

sneakers

Then **Jack gets dressed**.

16

What might **Jack** and his **rabbit** do during the **day**?
You choose…

trains

flag

den

Do they **play** with the **trains**
in the **morning**…

or do they
scoot in
the **park**?

scooter

Do they **build** a **den**
in the **afternoon**…

cake

or do they **bake**
a **cake**?

nighttime

bath time

bath

At the end
of the **day**,
it's time for
a **bath**. Then
it's **bedtime**.

bedtime
snuggle

pajamas

Jack and his **rabbit** like to
snuggle at bedtime.

slippers

17

Around the house

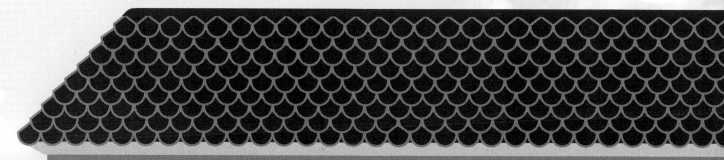

bedroom

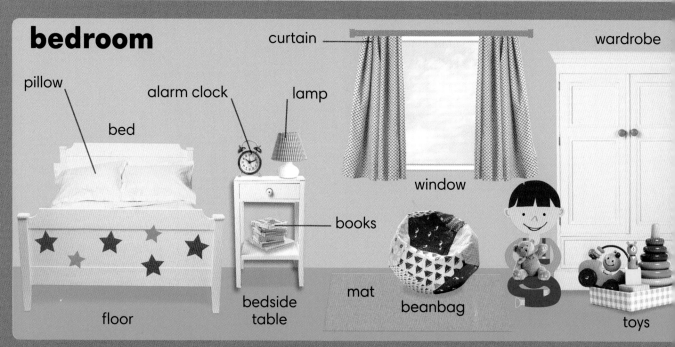

pillow

bed

alarm clock

lamp

curtain

wardrobe

window

books

mat

beanbag

floor

bedside
table

toys

kitchen

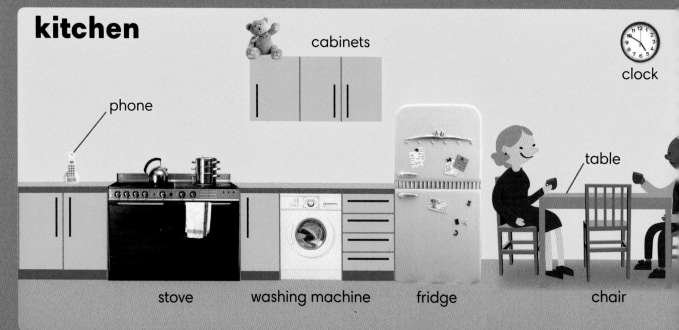

cabinets

clock

phone

table

stove

washing machine

fridge

chair

Choose a **cozy place** to read a book.

chimney

roof

bathroom

light

mirror

faucet

towel

shower

bathtub

sink

toilet paper

toilet

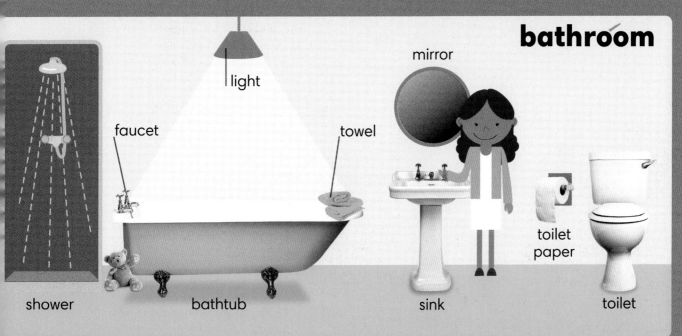

living room

door

picture

cushion

television

potted plant

side table

sofa

bookcase

doormat

steps

Toys and playtime

Which toy has a **long**, **spiky tail** and which one has **big, soft ears**?

tiara

firefighter helmet

balloons

kite

tepee

princess costume

firefighter costume

ball

doll

toy box

tambourine

train

train set

train track

dollhouse

rocking horse

marbles

fire engine

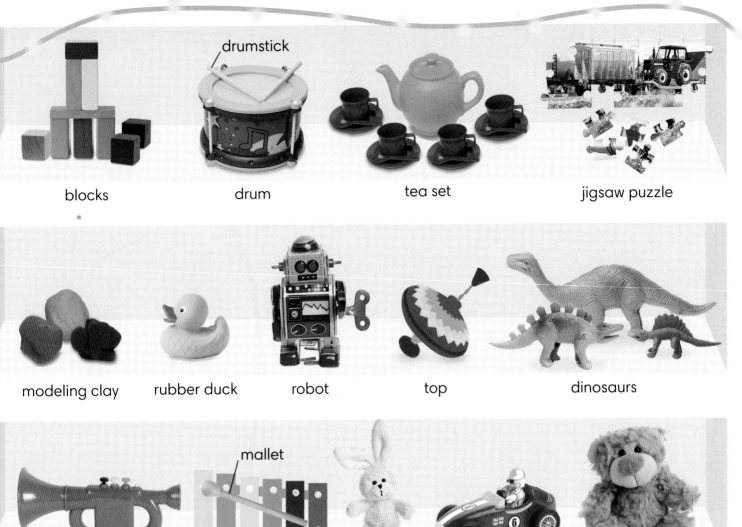

blocks

drumstick

drum

tea set

jigsaw puzzle

modeling clay

rubber duck

robot

top

dinosaurs

mallet

trumpet

xylophone

rabbit

car

teddy bear

pencils

pens

paper

paintbrushes

paints

books

I can...

read a book

draw pictures

play with a toy

play music

dress up

21

In the kitchen

scale

storage jars

rolling pin

faucet

vegetable peeler

chopsticks

kettle

dishwashing liquid

fork

plate

sink

knife

spoon

sponges

dish towel

colander

cereal bowl

mop

bucket

dustpan and brush

cake pan

sieve

22

cup and saucer

glass jug

wooden spoon

whisk

herbs

sharp knife

chopping board

mug

toaster

frying pan

mixing bowl

grater pot cookie cutters

In the kitchen we...

prepare food

cook meals

bake cakes and treats

wash dishes

clean

set the table

eat

drink

Find something **spotted** and something **striped**.

23

Favorite pets

Which **pet** would you like to **care for**?

parakeet

birdcage

goldfish

fish tank

hamster wheel

hamster

hamster cage

collar

pet carrier

cat

dog

puppy

guinea pig

hutch

dog bed

rabbit

spinach leaves

dog bowl

toy bone

hay

toy mouse

kitten

cat bowl

lead

Tink's story

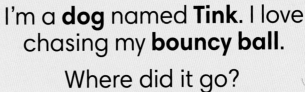

I'm a **dog** named **Tink**. I love chasing my **bouncy ball**.
Where did it go?

bouncy

ball

Tink

Is it **by** the **sleepy cat**?

Is it **on top** of the **hutch**?

rabbit hutch

rabbit

sleepy cat

Is it **in** the **sandbox**?

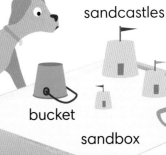

sandcastles

bucket

sandbox

shovel

bench

Is it **under** the **bench**? Yes!

ball

happy Tink!

friendly pup

Woof! Woof! Look who's come to play **ball** with me.

In the yard

snail

branch

fence

shed

birdhouse

bird

bush

broom

tree trunk

hose

lawn

petal

wheelbarrow

bee

ladybug

watering can

lawn mower

leaf

roses

trowel

spider

fly

gardening gloves

bulbs

26

web

rosebud

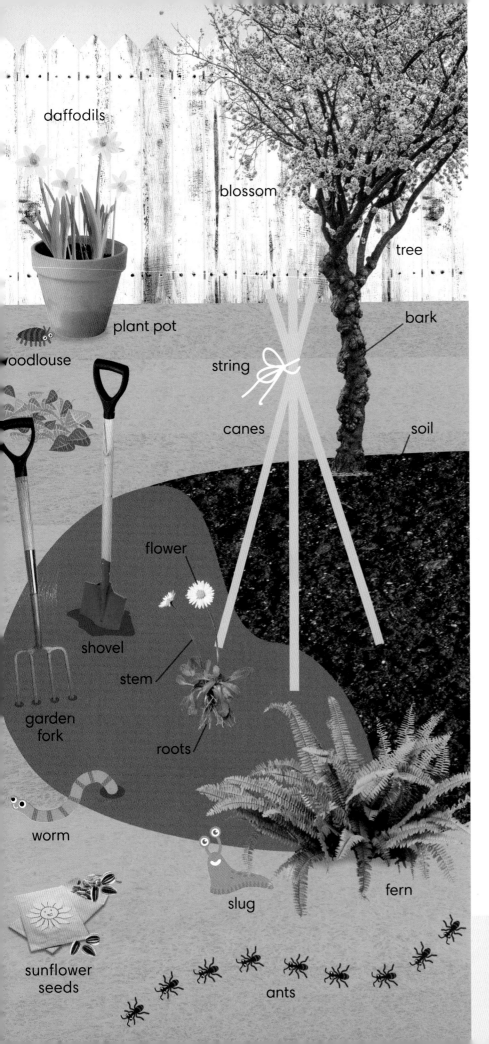

daffodils

blossom

tree

plant pot

bark

woodlouse

string

canes

soil

flower

shovel

stem

garden fork

roots

worm

sunflower seeds

slug

fern

ants

dig soil

plant seeds and flowers

water the plants

mow the lawn

sweep up leaves

Which garden creature has **eight legs**?

Describing people

young people

baby · child · kid · adolescent

toddler · boy · girl · teenager

grown-ups

adult · adult · adult

man · woman · old person

Eyes can be…

gray · brown · green · blue · hazel

Hair can be…

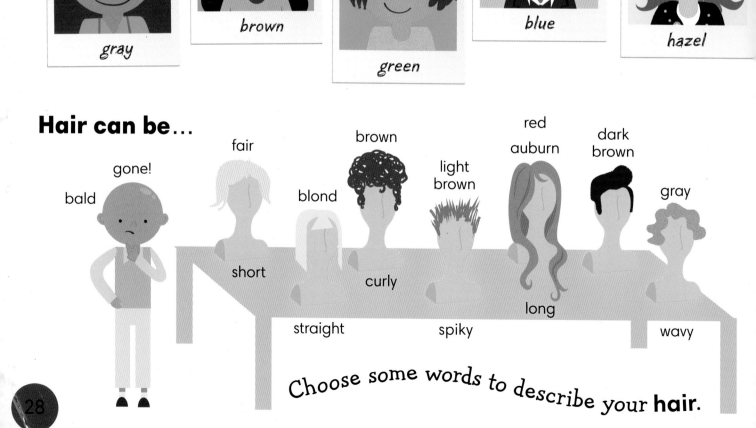

bald · gone! · fair · brown · light brown · red auburn · dark brown · gray

short · curly · straight · spiky · long · wavy

Choose some words to describe your **hair**.

In the country

birds

mountain bikers

hikers

trail

gate

hedge

tent

fox

camper

burrow

Campsite

sticks

bee's nest

kayak

flowers

bee

dragonfly

bud

eggs

pine cone

horse chestnuts

wild mushroom

tadpole

What contains the seed of an oak tree?

30

cloud

sky

sun

mountain

bird of prey

climber

waterfall

hill

trees

bird's nest

hare

bridge

stream

squirrel

river

wasp

frog

grass

eggs

caterpillar

chrysalis

butterfly

acorn

soil

froglet

What does a tadpole turn into?

In the city

Choose a place you would like to **visit**.

fountain

veterinarian's office

theater

movie theater

takeout restaurant

mall

bakery

shoppers

market

synagogue

construction site

police station

doctor's office

bank

hospital

restaurant

museum

butcher

dentist

grocery store

road

taxi

bench

beach

32

parking lot

temple

airport

runway

supermarket

library

skyscraper

town hall

train station

bouncy castle

slide

swing

park

statue

church

mosque

school

bridge

candy store

optician

café

houses

apartments

toy store

sidewalk

bus stop

Where could you go for some **food**?

33

Let's play school

Little Ted walks to **school** with her **dad**.

Dad

Little Ted

Her **teacher** smiles and says **he**

Hello

Little Ted

hooks

backpack

coat

teacher

Little Ted hangs up her **coat** and **backpack**.

song time

drum

triangle

Everyone sings a **good morning song**.

reading

letters

writing

abc

Then it's time for **reading** and **writing**.

After that, **Little Ted** paints a **picture**.

picture

painting

easel

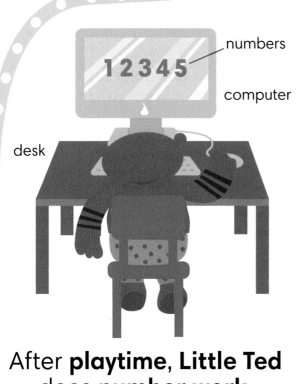

numbers

1 2 3 4 5

computer

desk

After **playtime, Little Ted** does **number work**.

Next it's **playtime**.

jumping

hopscotch

friends

Little Ted

teacher

Bye-bye

Then it's time to go **home**.
Little Ted has made some **friends**.

Around the farm

crow

fence

tractor with plow

farmer

soil

sheep

lambs

barn

fields

farmer

sheepdog

turkey

turkey chick

tractor

owlet

barn owl

chicken coop

chicks

stable

hen

peacock

donkey

horse

eggs

rooster

foal

hay

farmer

Let's name all the **baby animals** we can see.

wild rabbits

Find three **farmers**.

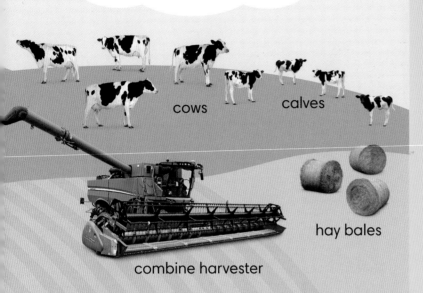

cows

calves

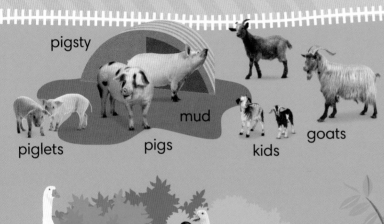

hay bales

combine harvester

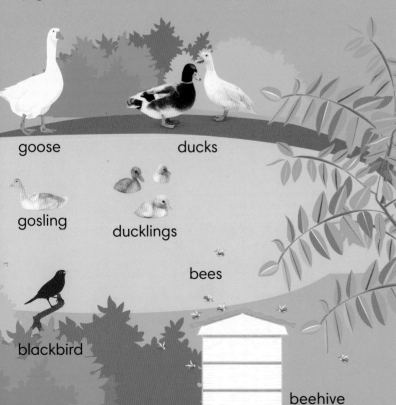

pigsty

piglets

pigs

mud

kids

goats

goose

ducks

gosling

ducklings

bees

blackbird

beehive

rice plants

olives

corn

wheat

apples

pears

coffee beans

tea plants

pineapples

bananas

37

Animals in the wild

giraffe

seagull

parrot

deer

chimpanzee

rhinoceros

lion cubs

lion

elephant

kiwi

jaguar

camel

elephant calf

tortoise

zebra

hippopotamus

panda
cub

zebra foal

mouse

Choose your favorite
furry animal and...

eagle

bat

snake

koala

monkey

moth

gorilla

cheetah

bear

bear cub

spider

lizard

kangaroo

joey

ostrich

tiger

flamingo

tiger cub

frog

wolf

leopard

cricket

your favorite
feathery animal.

beetle

39

River and lake animals

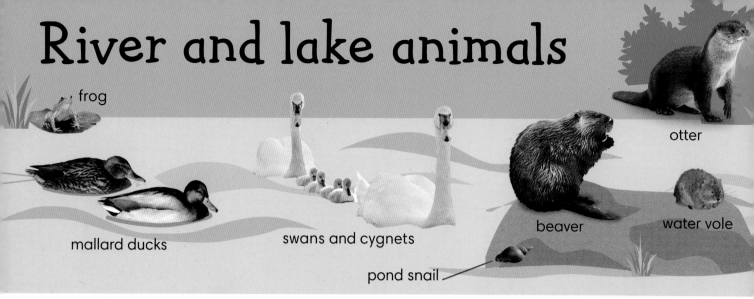

frog

otter

mallard ducks

swans and cygnets

beaver

water vole

pond snail

Find some animals with scales and...

Sea animals

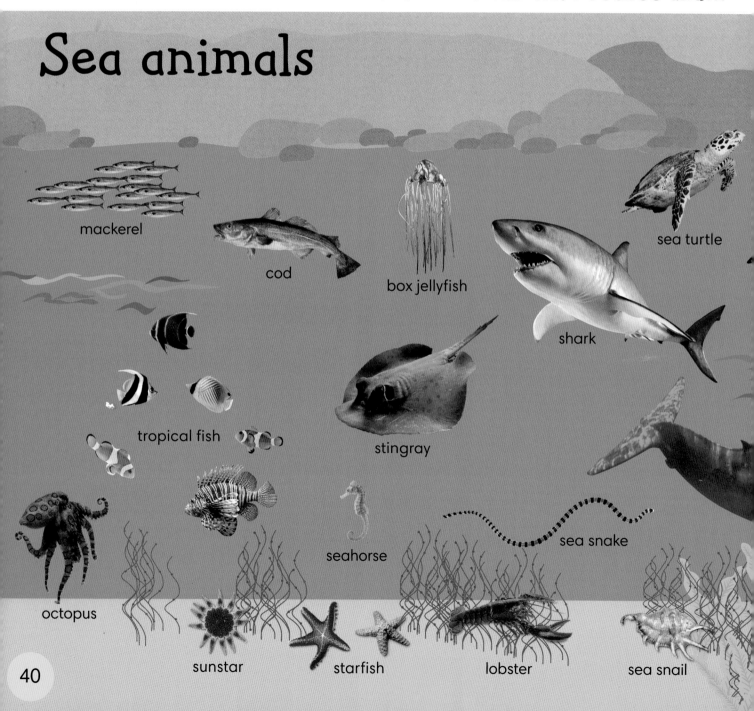

mackerel

cod

box jellyfish

sea turtle

shark

tropical fish

stingray

octopus

seahorse

sea snake

sunstar

starfish

lobster

sea snail

newt

alligator

crocodile

freshwater crab

crayfish

carp

fry

adult trout

eggs

a word for a **baby fish**.

penguin

sea lion

seal

orca

dolphin

beluga whale

blue whale

clam

razor clam

shrimp

saltwater crab

41

Full speed ahead!

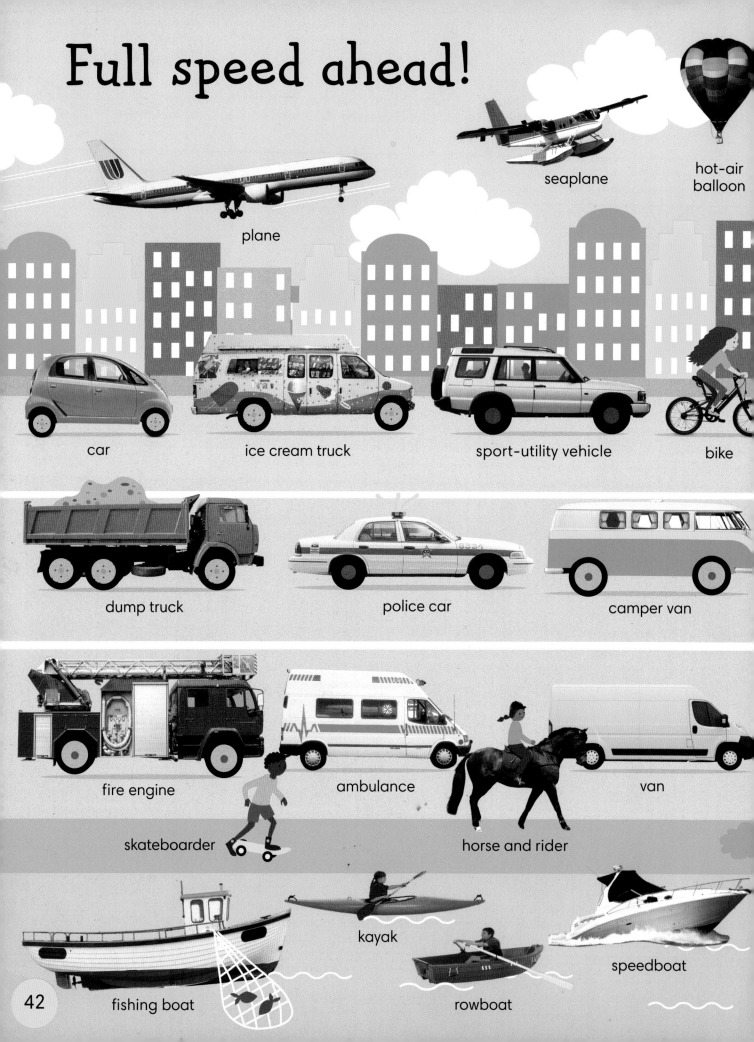

seaplane

hot-air balloon

plane

car

ice cream truck

sport-utility vehicle

bike

dump truck

police car

camper van

fire engine

ambulance

van

skateboarder

horse and rider

kayak

speedboat

fishing boat

rowboat

42

Should we **drive**, **fly**, or **float** in a boat?
Choose a **vehicle** you would like to **travel** in.

biplane

rescue helicopter

glider

garbage truck

motorcycle

race car

train

tractor

truck

digger

cement mixer

bus

motor scooter

runner

scooter rider

rescue boat

sailboat

ferry

Where will we go?

Daisy and Joe are going on a trip to Grandma's house.

They set off in a **taxi**...

luggage

taxi

home

to the **train station**.

then arrive at **Grandma's**.

train station

train

Grandma's house

What places might **Daisy** and **Joe** visit with **Grandma**? You choose.
(Look on the next page.)

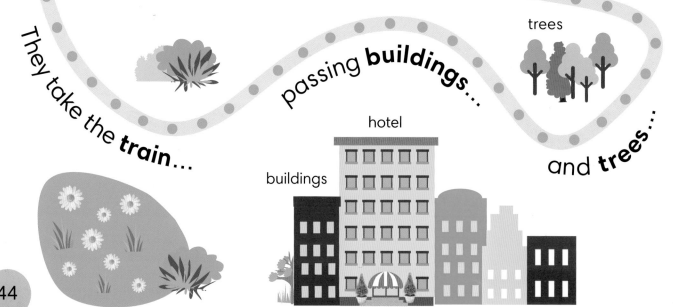

They take the **train**...

passing **buildings**...

and **trees**...

trees

hotel

buildings

swimming pool

carnival

zoo

aquarium

duck pond

Noisy animal words!

What people do

What **job** would you like to do?

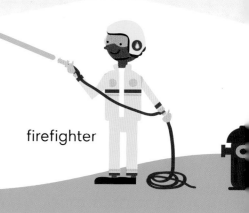
firefighter

doctor

nurse

fashion designer

singer

scientist

musician

dentist

DJ (disc jockey)

artist

hairdresser

actor

astronaut

builder

teacher

librarian

pilot

vet

film director

soccer player

chef

soldier

lawyer

athlete

dancer

police officer

babysitter

tennis player

engineer

president

writer

Some hobbies

gymnastics

martial arts

music

dancing

swimming

All sorts of places

moon

comet

Cold place

igloo

ice fishing

polar bear

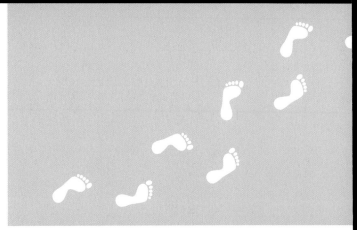

Imagine you are on an **adventure**.

Where will you **go**?

Savanna

lions

antelope

grasses

Ocean

diver

coral

fish

shipwreck

shark

seabed

stars

sun

space shuttle

Earth

Space

rocket

Desert

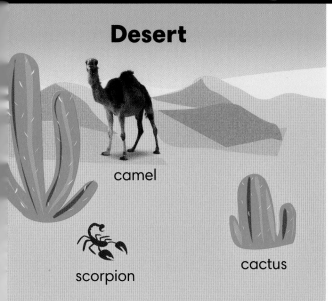

camel

scorpion

cactus

ree

parrot

tarantula

web

Rain forest

Some land and shore features

mountains

valley

lake

island

volcano

beach

cliff

estuary

51

Colors, shapes, and numbers

Colors

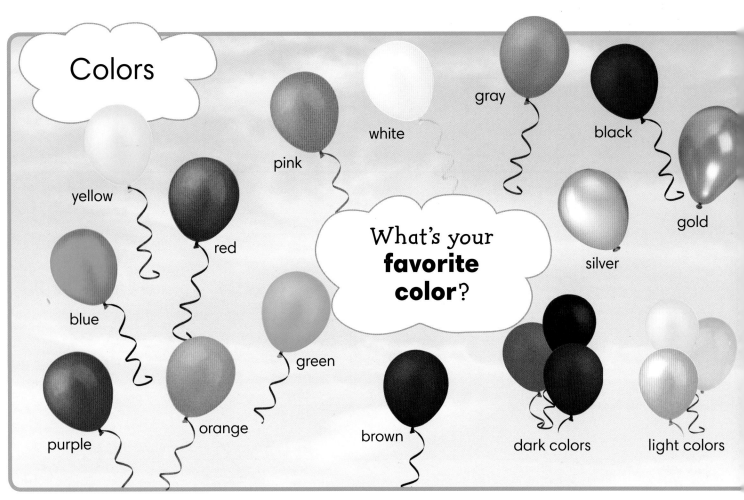

What's your **favorite color**?

yellow
pink
white
gray
black
red
silver
gold
blue
green
purple
orange
brown
dark colors
light colors

Shapes

Which shape is **round**?

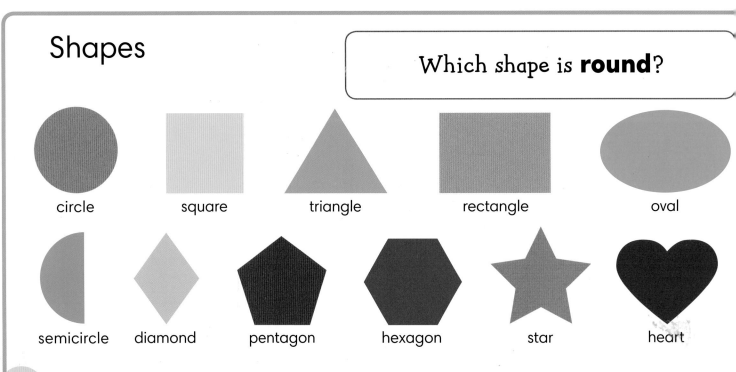

circle
square
triangle
rectangle
oval

semicircle
diamond
pentagon
hexagon
star
heart

Numbers

How many **green leaves** can you see?

0 zero

1 one

2 two

3 three

4 four

5 five

6 six

7 seven

8 eight

9 nine

10 ten

11 eleven

12 twelve

13 thirteen

14 fourteen

15 fifteen

16 sixteen

17 seventeen

18 eighteen

19 nineteen

20 twenty

100 one hundred

1000 one thousand

1000000 one million

Time, seasons, and weather

daytime   nighttime

Days

Monday

Tuesday

Wednesday

Thursday

Friday

Saturday

Sunday

Months

January

February

March

April

May

June

July

August

September

October

November

December

Seasons

Spring

Summer

Fall

Winter

What **month** is your **birthday**?

Some celebrations

Birthdays

 Diwali

Hanukkah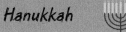

Eid

 Christmas

Chinese New Year

54

Weather

hot

sunny

cold

snowy

wet

rainy

dry

blue skies

rainbow

puddles

thunder and lightning

stormy

cloudy

breezy

windy

hail

foggy

frosty

icy

blizzard

 What's the **weather** like today?

Story time

fairy

unicorn

witch's cat

witch

broomstick

fairy godmother

alien

crown

palace

servant

cauldron

princess

prince

queen

king

toad

mouse

horse and carriage

glass slipper

wand

wolf

superhero

explorer

beast

wizard

bad guy

cave

Who rides a broomstick? Who wears a crown?

giant

genie

lamp

monster

magic carpet

castle

ghost

armor

sword

knight

shield

dragon

tower

spy

dinosaur

pirate

parrot

pirate ship

treasure

beanstalk

mermaid

coins

treasure chest

Let's make up a story

The beginning
Once upon a time...
(now choose a character)

or

a superhero...

a brave knight...

What happens to them?
You choose.

ice

is **frozen** in ice.

falls asleep and can't wake up.

microphone

can't stop **singing**.

apple

big

small

tiny

eats an apple and **shrinks**.

58

Who do they meet?

You choose. Along comes...

a **kind witch**.

a **helpful robot**.

rebooting machine

What happens next?

The robot's **rebooting machine** puts everything right.

wand

spell book

A **magic spell** puts everything right.

How does it end?

magical palace

happy friends

They live **happily ever after** in a **magical palace** with all their friends.

Wonderful words!

Have you ever **wondered**...

what words are?

We hear words as **sounds**.

hello!

We write them using **symbols**

dog

In English the symbols are called **letters**.

what words are for?

All words **mean** something.

apple

Apple means a crunchy, juicy fruit that's round and grows on a tree.

what words do?

Words do **different jobs** in a sentence.

Words that **name** things are called **nouns**.

Can you find these **nouns** in this book?

girl   tractor   moth   toad   ice cream

Words that tell you what something is **doing** are called **verbs**.

Can you find these **verbs** in this book?

walk   draw   seeing   jumping   tasting

Words that **describe** what something is like are called **adjectives**.

Can you find these **adjectives** in this book?

wet   curly   strong   happy   bouncy

Acknowledgments

The publisher would like to thank the following for their kind permission to reproduce their photographs:

(Key: a=above; b=below/bottom; c=center; f=far; l=left; r=right; t=top)

5 Dreamstime.com: Mikelane45 (clb). **6 123RF.com:** Rawan Hussein | designsstock (fclb/ice cream, fcr); Sataporn Jiwjalaen (ca); Ruslan Iefremov / Ruslaniefremov (fcra). **Dorling Kindersley:** Natural History Museum, London (fcl/butterfly); Tata Motors (fcla, fbl/Nano); Gary Ombler / Lister Wilder (clb). **Dreamstime.com:** Jessamine (fbl, crb). **7 Dorling Kindersley:** Natural History Museum, London (fclb); Tata Motors (bc). **8 123RF.com:** 6440925 (fbl); Belchonock (bc/Sun screen); Pixelrobot (fbr); Kornienko (bc). **Dreamstime.com:** Georgii Dolgykh / Gdolgikh (br). **10 123RF.com:** Piotr Pawinski / ppart (fcla/Green, fcl/Red, fclb/Brown, fclb/Purple). **10-11 Dreamstime.com:** Fibobjects (b/Flowers). **11 123RF.com:** Piotr Pawinski / ppart (tr/Grey, cr/Blue); Anatolii Tsekhmister / tsekhmister (tr). **Dreamstime.com:** Piyagoon (crb). **Fotolia:** Fotojagodka (tr/Cat). **12 123RF.com:** Murali Nath / muralinathpr (clb); Punkbarby (fcl). **Dreamstime.com:** Milos Tasic / Tale (clb/Sport Shoes). **13 123RF.com:** Burne11 (tc); Natthawut Panyosaeng / aopsan (ca); Sataporn Jiwjalaen (bc). **Dreamstime.com:** Chiyacat (cra). **iStockphoto.com:** Tarzhanova (fcra). **14 123RF.com:** Angelstorm (cra/Strawberries); Rose-Marie Henriksson / rosemhenri (fcrb/Cupcakes); Belchonock (bc/Celery). **Dreamstime.com:** Tracy Decourcy / Rimglow (fcr/Carrot); Leszek Ogrodnik / Lehu (cra/Apple, fcra/Orange, c/Red Pepper, cb/Broccoli, crb/Cabbage); Elena Schweitzer / Egal (cra/Cauliflower, bc/Lettuce); Grafner (br). **15 123RF.com:** Karammiri (clb); Utima (fbl). **Alamy Stock Photo:** Peter Vrabel (br). **Dreamstime.com:** Denlarkin (fclb); Tarapatta (ca); Pogonici (cla/Yogurt). **17 123RF.com:** Evgeny Karandaev (tl). **18 123RF.com:** Andriy Popov (cb). **18-19 Dreamstime.com:** Hai Huy Ton That / Huytonthat (b). **19 Dreamstime.com:** Jamie Cross (crb); Svetlana Voronina (ca); Kettaphoto (clb). **20 Dreamstime.com:** Stephanie Frey (cr); Thomas Perkins / Perkmeup (crb). **21 123RF.com:** Birgit Korber / 2005kbphotodesign (c). **Dorling Kindersley:** Toymaker, Jomanda (fcr). **Dreamstime.com:** Thomas Perkins / Perkmeup (fbr). **24 Dreamstime.com:** Photka (br). **26-27 123RF.com:** Leo Lintang (t). **Dreamstime.com:** Hai Huy Ton That / Huytonthat. **26 123RF.com:** Dmitriy Syechin / alexan66 (clb, bl); Singkam Chanteb (ca). **Dreamstime.com:** Aprescindere (bc, bc/Rose); Fibobjects (cra); Aleksandar Jocic (c); Danny Smythe / Rimglow (crb). **AA Photolibrary:** Stockbyte (cla). **27 123RF.com:** Lev Kropotov (tc); Keatanan Viya (cb). **Dreamstime.com:** Andreykuzmin (c); Andrzej Tokarski (cl). **30 123RF.com:** Sergey Kolesnikov (cb); Oksana Tkachuk / ksena32 (clb). **Dreamstime.com:** Steve Allen / Mrallen (cra/Kelp Gull); Liligraphie (cra); Sergey Uryadnikov / Surz01 (tr); N Van D / Nataliavand (clb/Poppy); Isselee (br). **30-31 Fotolia:** Malbert. **iStockphoto.com:** T_Kimura (t). **31 123RF.com:** Oksana Tkachuk / ksena32 (cla, cb). **Dreamstime.com:** Stephanie Frey (cra); N Van D / Nataliavand (cl, c, clb); Stevenrussellsmithphotos (crb). **iStockphoto.com:** Aluxum (clb/Frog). **36 123RF.com:** BenFoto (crb/Peacock); Ron Rowan / framed1 (br, br/Rabbit). **Dorling Kindersley:** Philip Dowell (cla, cla/Sheep). **Dreamstime.com:** Anagram1 (tr); Eric Isselee (clb); Jessamine (bl); Oleksandr Lytvynenko / Voren1 (bc/Chicken); Goce Risteski (ca); Photobac (crb). **37 123RF.com:** Eric Isselee / isselee (cla); Eric Isselee / isselee (cla/Veal); Alexey Zarodov / Rihardzz (cra/haystack). **Dorling Kindersley:** Alan Buckingham (cr); Doubleday Swineshead Depot (ca/Combine Harvester). **Dreamstime.com:** Eric Isselee (cla/cow); Eric Isselee (c); Yphotoland (crb); Just_Regress (cra); Damian Palus (ca). **Fotolia:** Eric Isselee (ca/cow). **Getty Images:** Dougal Waters / Photographer's Choice RF (br). **38 123RF.com:** Duncan Noakes (cl); Andrejs Pidjass / NejroN (tc); Ana Vasileva / ABV (c). **Dorling Kindersley:** Andrew Beckett (Illustration Ltd) (cr); British Wildlife Centre, Surrey, UK (cra/Deer). **Dreamstime.com:** Justin Black / Jblackstock (br); Eric Isselee / Isselee (fcl); Cynoclub (bc); Isselee (fcra). **Fotolia:** Eric Isselee (cla/Lion Cubs); Valeriy Kalyuzhnyy / StarJumper (tl); shama65 (cra); Eric Isselee (fbl); Eric Isselee (bc); Jan Will (fbr). **39 123RF.com:** Vitalii Gulay / vitalisg (ca/Lizard); smileus (cr); Александр Ермолаев / Ermolaev Alexandr Alexandrovich / photodeti (tc); Alexey Sholom (cl). **Dorling Kindersley:** Natural History Museum, London (cra/moth). **Dreamstime.com:** Hel080808 (crb); Brandon Smith / Bgsmith (ca); Goinyk Volodymyr (tr); Ryan Pike / Cre8tive_studios (cla); Kazoka (cb); Valeriy Kalyuzhnyy / Dragoneye (clb). **Fotolia:** Eric Isselee (tr/Koala); Eric Isselee (bc). **Photolibrary:** Digital Vision / Martin Harvey (clb/Tige Cub). **40 Alamy Stock Photo:** Rosanne Tackaberry (fcla). **Dorling Kindersley:** Weymouth Sea Life Centre (fclb). **Dreamstime.com:** Andybignellphoto (fcra); Paul Farnfield (ca); Jnjhuz (ca); Isselee (fcl); Elvira Kolomiytseva (cb); Cynoclub (clb/Lionfish); Veruska1969 (bc); Ethan Daniels (crb); Berczy04 (br); Richard Carey (cr). **iStockphoto.com:** Alxpin (clb). **41 Alamy Stock Photo:** WaterFrame / Blue Whale. **Dreamstime.com:** Tom Ashton (cra); Matthijs Kuijpers (tc); Chinnasorn Pangcharoen (tr); Margo555 (cla); Lext (ca); Vladimir Blinov (fcla); Snyfer (ca/Sea lion); Isselee (cra/Seal); Musat Christian (fcl); Caan2gobelow (cr). **iStockphoto.com:** Cmeder (cb). **42 123RF.com:** Gary Blakeley (br/Speedboat); Veniamin Kraskov (cl); Somjring Chuankul (clb); Kzenon (crb). **Dorling Kindersley:** Tata Motors (cla). **Dreamstime.com:** Maria Feklistova (tc); Melonstone (bl). **43 123RF.com:** Artem Konovalov (cr); Nerthuz (cla). **Corbis:** Terraqua Images (cr). **Dorling Kindersley:** Hitachi Rail Europe (fcra). **Dreamstime.com:** Eugenesergeev (br); Shariff Che\' Lah (cra); Mlan61 (cb). **New Holland Agriculture:** (fcl). **44 123RF.com:** Scanrail (clb/Train). **Dorling Kindersley:** Andy Crawford / Janet and Roger Westcott (cr/Car); Tata Motors (tr). **Dreamstime.com:** Fibobjects (bl, cra). **45 123RF.com:** Acceptphoto (clb/Llama). **Alamy Stock Photo:** Rosanne Tackaberry (crb/Duck). **Dorling Kindersley:** Andy Crawford / Janet and Roger Westcott (tl). **46 123RF.com:** Lev Dolgachov (fclb); Olaf Schulz / Schulzhattingen (c). **Dreamstime.com:** Fotomirc (bc/Rooster); Jmsakura / John Mills (cr); Eric Isselee (bc); Isselee (br). **Fotolia:** Malbert (cb/Water). **Getty Images:** Don Farrall / Photodisc (cb). **46-47 Dreamstime.com:** Glinn (b). **47 Dorling Kindersley:** Odds Farm Park, Buckinghamshire (ca/Pig). **Dreamstime.com:** Anna Utekhina / Anna63 (bl); Maksim Toome / Mtoome (cla); Yudesign (tc); Uros Petrovic / Urospetrovic (fcra); Eric Isselee (fcra/Cow); Chris Lorenz / Chrislorenz (ca); Rudmer Zwerver / Creativenature1 (fclb); Mikelane45 (clb); Jagodka (bc). **50 Dorling Kindersley:** Greg and Yvonne Dean (crb); Jerry Young (cra). **51 Dreamstime.com:** Ali Ender Birer / Enderbirer (tl). **52 Dreamstime.com:** Alinamd (t); Snake3d (cra). **53 123RF.com:** Dmitriy Syechin / alexan66 (cr); Jessmine (fcra). **Dreamstime.com:** Dibrova (fcr); Jlcst (cl); Ralf Neumann / Ingwio (cra); Irochka (c); Qpicimages (cr/Hibiscus leaf); Paulpaladin (cr/Mint Leaf). **54 123RF.com:** Mikekiev (r). **55 Dorling Kindersley:** Andy Crawford / Janet and Roger Westcott (bl). **56 123RF.com:** Eric Isselee (cla); Boris Medvedev (c). **Dreamstime.com:** Iakov Filimonov (cb); Alexander Potapov (cl/Shoe). **Fotolia:** Malbert (cl). **Getty Images:** C Squared Studios / Photodisc (ca). **56-57 iStockphoto.com:** Rodnikovay (b). **57 123RF.com:** Andreykuzmin (ca/Shield); Blueringmedia (b); Oliver Lenz (l); Konstantin Shaklein (cl); Jehsomwang (crb). **Depositphotos Inc:** mreco99 (cra). **Dorling Kindersley:** Wallace Collection, London (ca/Armour). **Fotolia:** Malbert (ca). **60 Dorling Kindersley:** Natural History Museum, London (cb). **Dreamstime.com:** Artigiano (crb/Strawberry); Grafner (crb). **New Holland Agriculture:** (cb/Tractor). **61 123RF.com:** Scanrail (fcra). **Dorling Kindersley:** Natural History Museum, London (fclb); Tata Motors (bc, fcrb). **Dreamstime.com:** Jessamine (bl, fcrb/Nest)

Cover images: *Front:* **123RF.com:** Parinya Binsuk / parinyabinsuk cb, Ruslan Iefremov / Ruslaniefremov clb/ (fountain), Scanrail cb/ (train); **Corbis:** Terraqua Images clb/ (helicopter); **Dorling Kindersley:** Natural History Museum, London tl/ (butterfly), Tata Motors tr; **Dreamstime.com:** Andygaylor clb, Borislav Borisov cb/ (bird), Jessamine tl/ (nest), Anke Van Wyk tl; **iStockphoto.com:** ZargonDesign cl; *Back:* **123RF.com:** Parinya Binsuk / parinyabinsuk cb, Rawan Hussein | designsstock cl/ (ice cream), Ruslan Iefremov / Ruslaniefremov clb/ (fountain), Sataporn Jiwjalaen / onairjiw tl/ (sunglasses), Scanrail cb/ (train); **Corbis:** Terraqua Images clb/ (helicopter); **Dorling Kindersley:** Natural History Museum, London cra, Tata Motors tr; **Dreamstime.com:** Andygaylor clb, Borislav Borisov cb/ (bird), Xaoc tl; **iStockphoto.com:** ZargonDesign cl

All other images © Dorling Kindersley
For further information see: www.dkimages.com

Keep learning words! They are very **useful**.

61